VOLCANOES

Cy Armour

Table of Contents

Volcano!

Long ago, people thought that powerful gods lived inside volcanoes. When the gods were angry, they would spit fire, ash, and lava onto the land.

Today, we know that volcanoes are a part of nature.

The word **volcano** comes from *Vulcan*, the Roman god of fire.

But why do volcanoes happen?

Why Volcanoes Happen

A volcano starts as a big, deep hole or crack in the earth. When pressure builds, ash, rock, gas, and **magma** escape through the hole. In time, the escaped material can form a mountain.

What Is It?
Magma (MAG-mə) is hot melted rock.

Why does this happen?

The earth is made of layers. The outside layer is the **crust**. The crust is made of big pieces of land called **plates**. The plates move slowly against one another.

Under the crust is the **mantle**. It is a thick, hot layer of rock. Deep inside the earth, it is so hot the rock melts into magma.

Pressure and heat in the mantle push the magma into a **magma chamber**. Magma is lighter than the crust, so it tries to push above it.

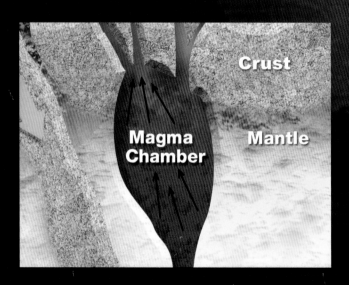

Crust

Magma
Chamber

Mantle

Finally, pressure from gases pushes the magma through the crust. This is called an **eruption**.

Lava

Magma

Plate edges are the best places for magma to escape. But if plates are thin enough, magma can push through other holes and cracks in the earth's crust.

Eruption!

An eruption happens when magma, ash, rock, and gases are released from a volcano. Sometimes an eruption comes in a blast. Sometimes it comes in a slow ooze.

If a volcano might erupt, it is called **active**. If we think it will not erupt now or in the future, it is called **dormant** (DOR-mənt). Dormant is another word for asleep.

Think what happens when you shake a can of soda. When you open it, the soda might blast out or just overflow down the sides. It depends on how much pressure has built up.

The more pressure, the
bigger the blast!

Once outside the volcano, magma is called **lava**. Lava can be fast and runny or slow and thick. Either way, the lava is hot, hot, hot! It can be as hot as 2012° F.

Where Are Volcanoes?

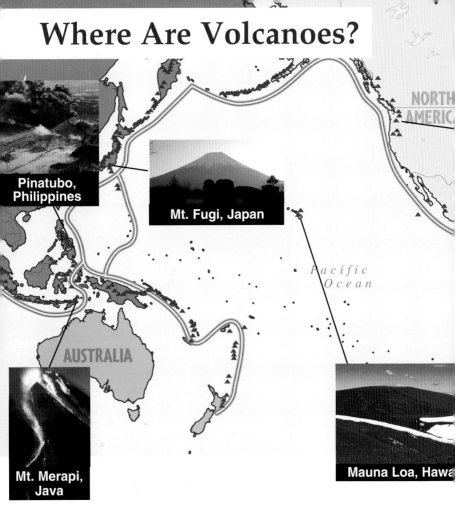

Pinatubo, Philippines

Mt. Fugi, Japan

Mt. Merapi, Java

Mauna Loa, Hawa

AUSTRALIA

NORTH AMERIC

Pacific Ocean

There are hundreds of volcanoes all over the world. More than half of them are along the shores of the Pacific Ocean. They are called the Ring of Fire.

Mt. St. Helens, Washington

Mt. Etna, Italy

EUROPE

AFRICA

SOUTH AMERICA

Atlantic Ocean

Indian Ocean

KEY

🔺 Active Volcano
〜 Ring of Fire
〜 Mid-Atlantic Ridge

Another large group of volcanoes is found under the Atlantic Ocean. It is called the Mid-Atlantic Ridge. It is the largest mountain range in the world!

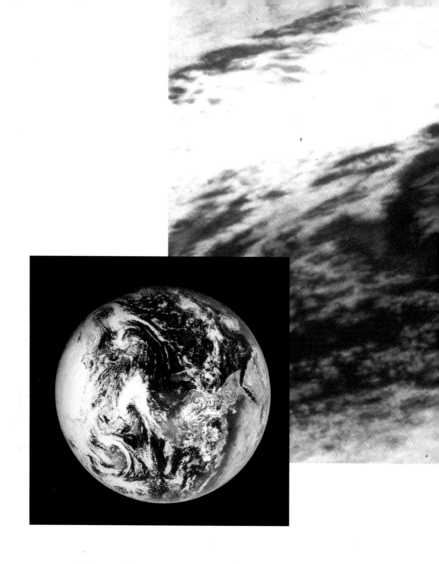

Earth is not the only place where volcanoes are found. They are on other planets, too.

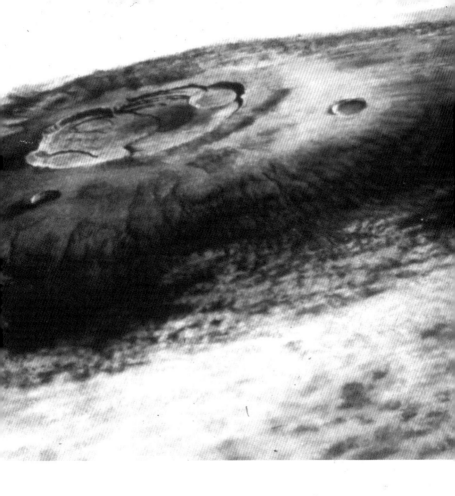

In fact, the largest volcano we know is Olympus Mons on Mars. It is 16 miles tall and as wide as all of Arizona.

Now that's a big volcano!

Glossary

crust   the top layer of Earth

eruption   the release of magma, ash, rock, and gases from a volcano

lava   magma that is outside a volcano

magma   hot, liquid rock

magma chamber   a pocket within a volcano where magma collects before erupting

mantle   a thick layer of Earth below the crust that is made of gas and magma

plates   large sections of Earth's crust that move, sliding together and apart

pressure   force that builds and pushes against something

volcano   areas of land where magma from inside Earth is pushed to the surface and out in an eruption